CONTEMPORARY COMMUNION MEDITATIONS

Fingerprints
on the
Chalice

CONTEMPORARY COMMUNION MEDITATIONS

Fingerprints on the Chalice

Steven E. Burt

C.S.S. Publishing Co., Inc.

Lima, Ohio

Fingerprints on the Chalice

Copyright © 1990 by
The C.S.S. Publishing Company, Inc.
Lima, Ohio

Library of Congress Cataloging-in-Publication Data

Burt, Steven E., 1949-
    Fingerprints on the chalice : contemporary Communion meditations /
by Steven E. Burt.
      p.   cm.
    "Originally published in Pulpit Digest, July-August, 1981"--
ISBN 1-55673-217-1
    1. Lord's Supper-- Meditations.   I. Title
BV825.2.B87   1990
234'.163--dc20

                                          89-49288
                                             CIP

9030 / ISBN 1-55673-217-1
                 PRINTED IN U.S.A.

Table of Contents

Taking Time to Love[1]

1 Corinthians 11:23-26

Describing Communion may be like describing the taste of a mango. It's different for everyone. When I try to reduce it to words, I'm limited to poetry or comparisions — describing what it's like, not what it is. But somehow I come back to the idea that it's a time when my spirit and God's touch, and we take time out to love.

1 Corinthians 11:23-26 is about a meal. It didn't take place in Rome, the focal point of the world at that time. It took place in Jerusalem, a city of captivity which would be destroyed forty years after the meal.

And the meal didn't take place in a palace or an inaugural ballroom. It happened in the upper room of a house of which we don't know the owner, the condition, or the location. Of the thirteen people present, only one had any sort of reputation, and he'd be dead the next day. The other twelve were young working class men whom nobody had ever heard of nor expected to ever hear from again. And no banquet. Just the basics of bread and drink.

So why is it that a simple, nondescript meal in a simple, nondescript place with thirteen rather simple, nondescript people in an out-of-the-way city off the main path of world affairs has been made the focal point of worship for millions of people for 2000 years? What made that meal Communion?

Have you ever noticed that the simplest events in life may turn out to be time-stoppers? Hasn't some little thing had a profound effect on your life and remained in your memory forever?

Fingerprints on the Chalice

It's the last supper, and I'm sitting at the end of the table, farthest from Jesus. It's pretty much like the end of any other week for us disciples. We're all exhausted. It's Thursday night, and we've been preaching and ministering and healing and teaching sixteen hours a day. Now it's time to relax a bit, talk over the exciting events of the week, and map out a strategy for the weekend.

Jesus is strangely quiet. Maybe he's more tired than any of us. He should be. I don't know where he gets his strength. I feel burned out. But Jesus just keeps going.

Just about everyone is talking in twos and threes now — except Jesus and except me. I'm really beat. If they all knew how really burned-out I'm feeling right now and how close I am to quitting this proclaiming-the-Kingdom-of-God, they'd pay attention to me. They're so busy ministering to the multitudes, the poor, the sick, the lame, the lepers. How about me? Who ministers to us disciples? Who ministers to us? Jesus can't be expected to do it all. God, I'm depressed.

Doesn't anybody care about me? So busy planning for our next campaign and so busy yakking about their minor little triumphs. What about me? Nobody's talking to me. They're just ignoring me. Am I not a person, too? God, help me.

It's not just inside this room either. Outside everybody's busy, busy, busy. It's Passover, and everyone's getting ready for the festival. Everybody's in town to celebrate our deliverance from the hands of the Pharaoh in Egypt.

And Pilate is in town. And Herod isn't far off. So there are political as well as religious goings-on. The town's buzzing. Nobody slows down for anybody else. They're all caught up in the frantic business of life.

I hope we eat supper soon. Maybe then I'll get a word in. There comes Jesus now. I knew they'd quiet down when he stood up. Why's he so quiet? You'd think it was his last meal or something. Jesus, say the blessing as you always do and break the bread as you always do.

He's looking right at me. It's as though he can see inside me. Did he say my name? "This is my body given for you." That's not our usual grace. Was that said to me? He did say my name.

It was for me. He knows how I feel. He does care.

I wonder if the others feel as I do. It's as if time is standing still. This is a strange, emotion-filled night. It's as though my spirit and God's are touching. Nobody's racing by, and the world isn't crashing in on us. My throat is in a knot. It's as if Jesus has stopped time by loving us.

I'm not worthy of his love, nor are any of us. If he only knew the foul-ups in my ministry — some of them so stupid I wouldn't dare tell him. And if he knew what I was thinking before the meal. God, help me.

New what? "New covenant in my blood." Why'd he say that to me? What does he mean by new covenant? I thought we had blown the old covenant long ago. We haven't kept our end of the deal with God.

And blood? That must mean sacrifice. Is he saying he's willing to sacrifice, to shed his blood for me? After all those sins I mentioned? After all those sins I didn't mention?

I can see sacrificing oneself for something of value. Lots of people will die for a good cause or a good person or a good friend. We'll die for something worth dying for. But why would anyone want to die for us? We're ungodly sinners. Nobody dies for something unless it's worth something. Except maybe God.

Did he say, "Do this in remembrance of me"? He said my name again. I heard it clear as day. What does he mean?

Here is the cup. What should I do with it? What does it mean? "Do this in remembrance of me." Do what? Eat? Drink? There's got to be more to it than that.

Maybe he means to do the same thing he's doing — not with the bread and the cup, but with his life — sacrificing his life for others. Maybe he means taking time out to love people as he's doing now. If he means sacrifice, does he mean my body, too? My blood? If I drink from this cup, am I sealing the covenant? Oh, God, help me.

Back to the present. It's like Jerusalem in many ways. I get wound up earning a living, ministering to people, trying to get ready for the holidays and relatives coming, attempting to be diplomatic in church and local politics. And sometimes I forget to take time to love and to be loved. And that may mean missing the simple little time-stoppers which can have a real impact on life.

My eight-year-old wrote a story for me, and she wanted me to read it. I was so caught up in hospital visiting, planning Sunday school lessons, and paying bills that I wanted to put her off. But she had written it primarily for me, and she wanted me to read it. So I stopped the world for a minute and read her story.

It was about the creation of the earth. A character named Peetle falls through a hole in a cloud. He falls and falls. Nothing for him to hit. So God sees his dilemma and quickly creates the earth, so Peetle can hit the earth, die, and return to heaven. The story showed me that my daughter knew it wasn't so important how the creation happened, but what was important was to know who did the creating. And I knew she loved me enough to take time to write a story for me. And she knew I loved her enough to take time to read it. We had communion.

In a YMCA basketball league for junior high boys, two teams came together — the first-place team and the last-place team. The first-place team was not only the best offensive team in the league, but also the best defensive team. Their coach took much pride in the fact that they had held their opposition to fewer than thirty points per game all year. They played like a well-oiled machine. And they were fast. When you watched their games, they just ran and ran, never slowing down. It's no wonder they were undefeated.

The other team was just the opposite. They lost every game. And when they played this first-place team, there was never any doubt about the outcome. No miracle story. The first-place team blew the last-place team out of the gym. They just ran and ran, never slowing their pace except once.

In YMCA basketball it's a rule that everyone on each team must get a chance to play. So at the start of the fourth quarter, when the game was far out of reach, both coaches began to substitute freely. And the first-place team's substitutes ran and ran, just as the starters had. And they played magnificent defense.

But there was one kid sitting on the end of the losers' bench who hadn't gotten to play yet. Finally, with about four minutes to play, the clock was stopped on an out-of-bounds play, and the coach put Jimmy in.

The clock started again and everyone was off and running. Even Jimmy. But it was obvious after two or three times up and down the court that Jimmy wasn't like all the other boys on the court. He was slower, not just physically but mentally, too. While the teams were racing one way for the basket, Jimmy was racing the other way.

Oh, he'd turn around eventually, but by then they'd be heading the other way again. And they'd run back and fourth with Jimmy caught somewhere in between.

Finally there came a time when both Jimmy and the teams were going in the same direction, and by mistake somebody threw the ball to Jimmy. Everything stopped. The officials froze. The crowd hushed. All the players stopped where they were. And this great defensive team, the pride of their coach for not allowing more than thirty points per game to be scored, stood still and dropped their hands to their sides.

Jimmy turned the ball in his hands a couple times, looked at the basket, took two or three steps without dribbling, and shot. He missed. But someone caught the ball and passed it back to him. And still no one moved. And Jimmy turned it in his hands again, looked at the basket, took two or three steps without dribbling and shot. The ball hit the rim and bounced in.

A roar went up, and Jimmy jumped up and down with glee. There wasn't a dry eye in the gymnasium. The clock stopped, another player came in, and Jimmy went back to the bench. The game went on, both teams racing and running until the final buzzer.

We don't know what will be meaningful and important in our lives. We keep rushing around, trying to attend to what we think are the important things, often putting people aside. We miss the times of communion when our spirits touch God's for a moment.

Nobody remembers what happened that Passover day outside the walls of the Upper Room. What we remember is a simple meal, significant to a band of disciples because love made time stand still. And there was communion.

And I really don't recall how the Sunday school lessons turned out, what checks I wrote, or what bills I paid. But I remember a simple story, significant to my daughter and to me because love made time stand still. And there was communion.

And nobody now remembers the final score of the basketball game, who fouled out, or who scored how many. But they all remember a simple encounter, significant to perhaps a hundred people because love made time stand still. And there was communion.

Let us take time from our busy schedules to attend to the loving relationship we have here with our Lord, Jesus Christ.

---

[1]Steven E. Burt, "Taking Time to Love," *Pulpit Digest*, July — August 1981, reprinted with permission.

Sunday Dinner with the Family of God

1 Corinthians 11:23-26

I remember my junior high school best friend, Bobby Hillman. Sad to say, he died of cancer about ten years ago. But I remember him. We had a lot of good times, played a lot of sports together. We talked a lot about life together. We ate a lot of meals together — in the school cafeteria, and in Paradise Sweets Shoppe after basketball games.

Bobby Hillman's father owned The Clothes Locker. It was a classy children's clothing store. Everything in it was fairly expensive because it was of high quality. My family never shopped there.

Bobby's mother didn't work, but she dressed. She was probably the best-dressed woman in town. And she wore makeup, wore it well. She was probably the best made-up woman in town. And her hair was always styled perfectly. She was probably the best coiffed woman in town. At least, in *my mind*, she was.

They always seemed to have a pretty new car; their house and lawn were well-kept. I heard rumors that the inside of the house was spotless, and that the furniture was never sat upon. I really didn't know, because it was years before they let me go past the back door into the house — since I usually smelled like the barn.

Finally, though, they let Bobby invite me to dinner one night. I remember feeling very nervous. It would be different.

Mrs. Hillman, who always spoke very politely but firmly, told us to go wash our hands before supper. Then we sat down at this elegant dining room table. White lace tablecloth. I was afraid I'd spill something on it and get yelled at.

Everyone had matching tumblers instead of jelly glasses. I was used to jelly glasses. The milk was in a pitcher, not in a bottle. And there was a fancy little dish for ketchup and another for mustard.

We had two forks each. I couldn't imagine why.

Each place setting had a cloth napkin, which I had previously seen at Easter, Thanksgiving, and Christmas dinners. (Our family always used to share a couple of dish towels.) It was fairly quiet, and what conversation there was tended to be stilted, because the adults did all the talking. I got the clear message that kids weren't to talk. Not much nonsense or superfluous conversation.

When anyone wanted anything, it was, "Please pass the butter?" The response: "Thank you." "You're welcome."

After supper I asked Bobby if it was always like that, and he said that that was a regular evening meal. I had survived it, but it was sure different from our supper table.

It wasn't long after that when I asked Bobby to come to our place for supper. He had been in and out of our house many times, because my mother had no restrictions. My dad once threatened to put in a revolving door to save on the heat loss and accommodate all the traffic.

Bobby had grabbed peanut butter and jelly sandwiches on the run for lunch at our kitchen from time to time, but he had never fully experienced a big meal with us.

We had hamburgers and rolls, French fries, corn on the cob. That was a fairly extravagant meal for us. It was me, my mother and father, my three sisters, my brother, and my two cousins from next door (who were often at our table). They practically lived with us. At any rate, it was a crowd around our kitchen round-table. (The dining room table was only used for special occasions like Thanksgiving or Christmas or Easter dinner.)

The noise level was fairly high, and behind us Mom was standing at the stove frying the hamburgers in two cast iron frying pans. She was doing the French fries in a kettle of grease over another burner, and had the corn on the cob in a big pot of water on the fourth burner. Between the talking, the French fries in the hot grease, and the sizzling hamburgers, it was noisy.

My friend Bobby Hillman looked stunned.

Then Mom put a plate of hamburgers and a plate of French fries down on the table.

They were gone before Bobby could make a move. In our farmhouse, at our kitchen table, it was every person for him or her self. (We eventually got some of the second batch.)

There weren't a lot of please-pass-the-butters or thank-yous or you're-welcomes. My mother encouraged such manners, but it didn't always happen. Instead, it was the sound of eating and talking, the airspace above the table filled with hands and arms reaching across in front of others or out into the middle of the table. Sometimes no more words than, "Salt!" or "Butter?"

One fork each, jelly glasses for everybody, ketchup bottles and mustard jars right there on the table.

it was sure different from the dinner we had shared in Bobby Hillman's dining room. But he survived it. I'm sure he came to our house with as much fear and trembling as I took to his.

Everything new and different. That isn't to say that it was right or wrong. It was just different. But we enjoyed a meal together. We shared the food and the experience.

I miss him. I miss my junior high school best friend, Bobby Hillman.

But somehow, over the Christmas holidays last year, when my in-laws were visiting, when we were sitting around the table sharing a meal, when everyone was sort of talking excitedly and grabbing ketchup and mustard — I realized that none of the glasses matched — and Bobby Hillman came to mind. He suddenly sprang to life in my heart and memory again. In the context of that holiday meal, in the context of that meal when he wasn't even present, Bobby was suddenly, momentarily, real. The meal, the setting, made him alive in my heart. It's funny what our minds can do.

Someone once said that what distinguishes human beings from animals is that we have the capacity to make meaning. *We are meaning-makers.* We're the ones who mint a dime and say, "That *stands for* ten pennies." Animals can't ascribe meaning to a coin that way.

We are the ones who design a flag and say, "When you see this flag, salute it, because it *stands for* our country." Animals can't ascribe meaning to a piece of cloth that way.

We are the ones who can write a wedding ceremony to unite two persons as life's companions. We say the words and they *mean* something. Animals can't write ceremonies.

We are the ones who can turn a tree into a Christmas tree, a band of gold into a symbol of commitment, a song into a national anthem.

But meaning isn't just something we *give*. Meaning is also something we *get*. We gain from it.

By giving meaning to our flag, we gain a sense of pride when our throats knot up and tears stream down our cheeks as we watch it raised over an American athlete who has taken first place at the Olympics. We gain because we have allowed that object to be meaningful in our lives.

Sometimes the meaning isn't tied to an object. It may instead be associated with a familiar ritual.

A funeral is a ritual that allows us to begin healthy grieving.

A family Thanksgiving dinner is a ritual that may have meaning for some of us. "Over the river and through the woods, to grandmother's house we go."

Ascribing meaning to certain objects and rituals allows the mysterious, the incomprehensible, the intangible to become somehow real to us.

The Viet Nam war becomes very, very real to those of us who weren't over there when we see "The Wall," the Vietnam Veterans' Memorial in Washington, D. C. The Wall isn't the war or the sacrifice. It's just a wall — but it's a powerful symbol that can conjure up incredible memories and emotion to affect our lives.

The reality of God's love may become visible to some of us when we see the Nativity drama acted out.

Seeing a work of art like the *Mona Lisa*, or singing Handel's *Messiah*, or receiving an award -- all of these, by allowing us to extract meaning, can make something invisible real.

That's what we're doing today. We're sharing a meal we call Communion or the Lord's Supper. We're sharing it not so much to get the food — there isn't that much bread on the plate — but to extract and share the meaning.

William Willimon, a professor at Duke, has written a book about Communion, and in it he refers to Communion as Sunday Dinner. What a marvelous image. We're all here like a family to share Sunday dinner.

We'll all be fed, of course. But something more will happen. The invisible, the intangible, the mysterious, will become somehow suddenly real. Some of us will experience the real presence of God. Others a sense of family. Still others a feeling of security, of belonging to something bigger than ourselves.

Fingerprints on the Chalice

Part of it may come from the ritual itself, from the repeating of it, and from the security that comes from doing something over and over, like feeding the birds every morning, or walking the dog, or going to work. Part of it may come from renewing a vow or a commitment, touching base with one's spirituality. Part of it may come from the meaning we draw from the objects themselves — symbols: the bread, the cup, the body, the blood, the thinking about Jesus' sacrifice.

And since the Communion of saints is our belief that Communion unites Christians everywhere — past, present, and future — some of us will find the Bobby Hillmans become real and alive in our hearts and memories. We may expect it, or it may catch us by surprise.

Some of us who come from different backgrounds, from different churches, may find the dinner table set a bit differently, may find the manners and customs a bit strange, the glasses a bit different — everything a bit more formal or perhaps less formal — but it is still a meal, still a chance to commune together, still a chance to be together with each other before God.

Please join me today at the Lord's table . . . for Sunday dinner . . . with the family of God.

Fingerprints on
the Chalice

Luke 22:14-20

A while ago, while at a three-day pastor's retreat, I over-heard two young pastors discussing what happens at Communion. One wanted to discuss transubstantiation and consubstantiation — that is, what actually happens to the bread and wine when the priest or minister pronounces that they are the body and blood of Christ. The second wanted to theorize about the effect the elements had on the worshippers when they took in the body and blood (or the bread and juice, if it wasn't actually transubstantiated.) I chose not to get into their discussion, but it's made me think about Communion again.

It seems to me that the weakness in their discussion was that they were trying to *standardize* things — to nail down exactly what happened to the bread everytime, and what happened to the juice every time, and what happened to each parishioner every time.

To be truthful, though, I don't think we all get a big bang out of Communion *every* time; our responses *aren't* standardized. Our response depends on our moods, on the weather, on our histories, on whether we're in our home congregation or with strangers; it depends on many, many things. And each person is different. So each experience of Communion is different.

I've discovered, since being involved with flesh-and-blood *people* in parishes (and not just philosophies, which were the focus in seminary), that it's harder now to discuss

Fingerprints on the Chalice

Communion in the abstract, because it's individual and personal. What I've discovered is: Communion is only communion when *people* are involved, people with real physical features, with bunions and bruises, with tempers and teardrops, with histories and heart-aches, people whose cars wouldn't start because they left the lights on, whose English muffins get stuck in the toaster just as mine do, who forget to spring ahead and fall back (and then arrive late for church — or is it early?), people who try hard to know God but can't seem to in the way their more saintly friends do, who want to follow the Golden Rule but find it hard to love their neighbor when the neighbor's dog hasn't read the Golden Rule and has defiled the front lawn.

In picturing Communion, I thought of *people* — people with big noses, people with fly away hair, people with strange eyes, people with wrinkles and birthmarks and warts; I remembered *people*; I imagined *people*, each person unique and individual. Let me paint a picture for you of a Communion that might be going on somewhere.

The minister stands behind the rail, looking like a judge in his black robe. He's short and overweight, but even so, the robe is too short for him; it barely hangs below his knees. He's sweating, and his heavy black glasses threaten to slip down his nose every time he leans forward to serve someone.

The first person is a lady with a scarf on her head. She looks like a *baboushka*, a Russian grandmother, or like a migrant worker preparing to pick melons in the hot California sun. But the woman is just a regular middle class working woman. Under the scarf there's no hair. She is bald as a billiard ball. From the chemotherapy. You see, she's had a mastectomy, a breast removed by surgery, the only way to deal with her cancer.

that neither is to be feared. In some way, if we come to commune, if we come seeking God — for whatever reason — like the father greeting the prodigal son, God will seek us; God will rush to meet us with open arms of love.

What, then, is Communion? It's whatever it is that happens when we get together and, in Christ's name, share the bread and the cup, and say: "This is my body, broken for you. Take, eat. This is my blood, shed for you. Drink of it, all of you."

Please join me at the Lord's table.

Who Holds the Keys to the Kingdom?

Luke 14:12-15

Not long ago I met with a student pastor whom I was supervising. He was serving a church in a nearby town. In our conversation we got to talking about *who* ought to be allowed to come up to the rail for Communion. It seems he had gotten into a disagreement with another pastor in that same town.

The other pastor said that no children should be allowed to receive Communion. The pastor I supervised thought it was OK.

I, being an astute supervisor, and knowing my supervisee was coming up for ordination interviews soon, didn't give him the answer. Instead, I asked what such a decision might be based on.

His first answer was *tradition* — that is, the Methodist churches which this pastor had attended had always served children. But that didn't mean *all* Methodist churches did.

His next answer was that the rules and regulations of his church, the United Methodist Church, encouraged it — at least, the pastor *thought* that was written somewhere in the Methodist *Book of Discipline*.

His next answer was a question. "Why shouldn't they be allowed to, especially if the children are members, or at least if they are baptized Christians and members of the family of God and the household of faith?"

"A good argument," I said. "But why didn't the other pastor buy it?"

My supervisee wasn't sure.

Finally I said, "Picture what it is you're doing when you, as a pastor, particularly as a pastor in a long white robe, preside over the sacrament or ordinance we call Communion or the Lord's Supper."

"I'm serving," he said.

"Yes, you are," I said. "But whose part are you acting out?"

"Jesus' part," the pastor finally said.

"Fine," I answered. "And if Jesus were calling people to supper at his table, whom would he invite?"

"He'd certainly invite children," the pastor answered quickly, adding, "He'd invite any Christian practicing the faith."

"Any *Christian*?" I pressed.

The young pastor gave me a puzzled look, so I continued, "How many *Christians* were at the Last Supper?"

"None," the pastor answered. "They were all Jews."

"That's right," I said. "But aside from that, if Jesus himself were offering the invitation to eat, whom would he call?"

The pastor scrunched up his face, and I said, "Let me rephrase the question. If Jesus himself were at the head of the table — doing the inviting — whom do you think he would *exclude?* Children? Jews? Blacks? Muslims? Unbaptized people? Whom would he turn away?"

That look of understanding, of sudden awareness, came over his face, and he said, "From what I know of Jesus, he wouldn't turn anyone away. After all, we're talking about a person who ate with tax collectors, prostitutes, and sinners."

"That," I said like a wise old supervisor, "is what you must base your decisions on — the knowledge which comes out of *your relationship* with Jesus Christ — not by the books or creeds or tradition. Speak out of that relationship, and you can speak with authority."

It was what is called a *teaching moment*, one of those times when a critical learning or bit of wisdom strikes someone's consciousness with great impact.

We, too, need to think about what this is we're acting out. What is this ceremony, this sacrament, this ritual we call the Lord's Supper, Communion, the Eucharist?

In Luke's gospel Jesus may give us a piece of the answer. It's not just a meal for insiders, as so many churches have tried to make it. It's not a dinner meeting of the Christian Club. It's the beginning of a picture, a vision, of the fullness of the Kingdom of God. It's a foretaste of glory divine, as the hymn says.

In Luke 14:12-15 Jesus clearly shows us that the Kingdom of God and the banquet table of God are not for a select few. In the story we hear that Jesus said to the man who had invited him, "When you give a dinner or a banquet, do not invite your friends or your brothers and sisters or your kinfolk or rich neighbors for they will invite you in return and you will be repaid. When you give a dinner or a banquet, invite the poor, the lame, and the blind, and you will be blessed, because they cannot repay you. *You will be repaid at the resurrection of the just.*"

When one who sat at table with him heard this, he said, "Blessed is he who shall eat bread in the Kingdom of God."

You see, the Kingdom of God — the vision of the future we read about in Scripture, when the wolf shall lie down with the lamb, when we shall beat our swords into plowshares, when justice shall roll down like floodwaters and righteousness like an everflowing stream — the Kingdom of God . . . is for all, not just for some.

Fingerprints on the Chalice

The Lord's Supper, the Communion table, isn't yet the fullness of the Kingdom of God, but it's a start. It's a place where everyone can gather — rich and poor, children and adults, black and red and yellow and white, male and female, blind and sighted, lame and walking. It's a place where we can gather in peace, around the table of Jesus Christ which gives us a glimpse of the banquet table of the Kingdom of God.

Maybe some of you saw the movie *Places in the Heart*, with Sally Field. It's set in the South, in Texas, in the 1930s. The movie is filled with varieties of prejudice. There is prejudice against women — and the man who sells cotton seed to Sally Field tries to sell her inferior seed for full price, expecting that she won't know the difference. There is prejudice against poor people — and the banker and others only reluctantly allow Sally Field credit. There is prejudice against the disabled — and a blind man is pushed around and taken advantage of when he tries to help his black friend. And there is prejudice against blacks — and four local businessmen hide beneath their Ku Klux Klan hoods and almost beat Sally Field's black hired man to death. In addition to prejudice, inequality, and injustice, there is marital infidelity. Sally Field's brother-in-law is cheating on Sally Field's sister, something which is eventually discovered. Also, Sally Field is left a widow right in the beginning of the movie because her husband is accidentally shot. The young black teenager (who shot him) receives no trial — just vigilante justice, and he is dragged to death behind a car bumper.

If you recall, sin is separation — distance between the two parties — brokenness in a relationship. Sin can be seen in the broken relationship between us and God, or in the broken relationship between us and our neighbor.

Prejudice is sinful because it creates that distance; infidelity is sinful because it creates that distance. The distance can also be created and magnified by death. *Places in the Heart* is filled with sin, separation, brokenness, distance. The reason I mention it now, though, is for its powerful last scene. It is almost a dream sequence. In fact, it is a bit hazy, probably shot with a fuzzy filter on the camera so it would appear dreamy.

The scene is a church, and the minister walks to the pews to pass the Communion cup. Each person serves the next. And in the scene are *all* the people from the film — Sally Field and her dead husband with the black teenager who shot him, Sally Field's kids and the blind man who had boarded with them, the four men who had been Ku Klux Klansmen and the black hired man whom they beat up, the unfaithful brother-in-law and his wife, the banker and the unscrupulous cotton gin owner. All those people with brokenness, sin, and separation in their relationships — yet they were there, *together*. But they weren't there for the Lord's Supper as we know it. They were there sharing the Lord's supper as it is in that time we envision, in that time we dream about, in that time we pray for — that time we call the fullness of the Kingdom of God.

Sure, it's a dream, a vision, the Kingdom of God. But we're being asked to begin imagining it here and now, to begin stepping toward that vision like in *Places in the Heart*, to begin trying to flesh it out at our Communion rail or table.

I think my pastor friend grasped a bit of truth that day.

"When you give a dinner, don't invite just friends, brothers and sisters, kinfolk, insiders. Invite the poor, the maimed, the blind. You will be repaid at the resurrection of the just. Blessed is the person who shall eat bread in the Kingdom of God."

This is the Lord's table, not mine, and he invites all who hunger in any way to join him and be fed.

The Kingdom of God Is Like . . . a Joke!

Luke 10:25-37

The story of the good Samaritan is perhaps the most misunderstood of all Jesus' parables. We've lost sight, over the nineteen centuries since Jesus told it, of its real impact. Since we're not familiar with the original context in which its hearers heard it, we've seen it reduced to a good neighbor story, a Boy Scout doing a good deed a day, a driver stopping to help a little old lady change a flat tire. The emphasis is on the good Samaritan, the one who stops to help. Although that's a wonderful value to impress on our young people — helping neighbors in need — that wasn't where the original focus was.

You see, the impact was on the hearers. They were suddenly exposed — very suddenly and abruptly exposed — to the reality, to the presence of the Kingdom of God. They had thought this Kingdom or rule of God in each person's life was *coming*, but when Jesus confronted them with parables such as this one, they found that it had arrived, had caught them off guard, caught them sleeping like the servants who didn't stay awake while waiting for their master to return.

First, let me say something about the Kingdom of God. The thing folks were waiting for was the coming of the Kingdom. You know, "Thy Kingdom come; thy will be done." In this case Kingdom means something like the kingship or the rule or the sovereignty of God in each person's life. And isn't that what we'd like to see? Each person in a relationship

33

with God as his or her ruler, each *voluntarily* serving God, each seriously seeking to do God's will?

Of course, there are other images that go along with the Kingdom of God. The lion will lie down with the lamb; we will beat our swords into plowshares and share our fields rather than fight over them; there will be peace, justice, righteousness. But it's all based on the whole of creation being in right relationship with the Creator. Obviously there are a lot of things that will have to change for that to be realized.

Where do Jesus and his parables come into this? Well, I think Jesus knew that people's thinking was in a rut. They thought that the pecking order was fixed and unchangeable, that there could be nothing new under the sun (as the writer of Ecclesiastes said). It was like our thinking when we organized this country. Only *men* could vote. Who would ever have thought there was anything wrong with that? It was assumed that women not having the right to vote was fixed, correct, acceptable. It took many decades for that to be challenged.

The same was true of slavery. For economic reasons, or for whatever other reasons, for the longest time many people believed that it was acceptable to *own* another person. That idea persisted until the Civil War and the Emancipation Proclamation.

Likewise, Jesus realized that his hearers thought the social order was fixed, set in stone, unchangeable. He realized they believed that the lion *had the right* to kill and eat the lamb. And when he realized the plight of his hearers, Jesus thought, "I can confront them with parables and show them there is another way to work out the lion/lamb relationship and other relationships — that the Kingdom of God is not just a dream, but that it is actually at hand, upon us, in our midst." So he used parables, little stories which kept the hearers' interest, then suddenly sprang a point on them, confronting them with the possibility of a new reality, a new creation, a new hope for the world.

Parables work like the punchline of a modern joke. For example, someone asks, "Have you heard the one about the dummy who said "No?" And before you can stop and think, you answer "No" — and you suddenly realize, all in a split second, that you're caught, that you *are*, in fact, the dummy who has said "No." The joke's on you. You're confronted with a new reality, because in the moment before you *weren't* a dummy, and suddenly you've proven that you *are*. Reality has changed in a split second. Things aren't as you thought they were.

In Zen Buddhism there's a word, a concept, *satori*. It means "the little point." It's got to do with staring, for example, at a rose or a fly on the wall as you meditate, concentrating on one tiny point in the universe. As Westerners, we'd figure that, if we want to understand the world and ourselves in relation to it, we'd look at the world, at the larger picture. But to the Easterner, one begins to understand oneself in relation to the world by *narrowing*, not by *widening*, one's focus. To the Easterner, narrowing the focus is like concentrating all the energy into a laser. There's more, not less, power. We see it in the *haiku* poem, a compressed image which is designed to unfold and reveal its meaning.

The *satori* then, is that moment of heightened awareness, that explosion of understanding, what we call the "Aha!" moment or the "Eureka!" experience that comes out of focusing on the little point. It's like a tightly compressed hand grenade of awareness exploding in the mind. That realization, that sudden awareness that the world can be different than it appears — that which Social Darwinists call the "natural order of things" can be changed, that there can be peace in a world of war and violence — that realization of the possibility of the *present* Kingdom of God is what Jesus confronts his hearers with. His parable *springs* it on them, and it leaves some of them with their heads spinning.

In the Parable of the good Samaritan, we must realize that the question is asked by a young lawyer, an expert on the religious law. He's wondering how far his obligation to "love your neighbor as yourself" must extend. In other words, tell me the persons I'm required to love so that I can inherit eternal life, and, by God, I'll be sure to love them. "Just give me a list, Jesus, and I'll fulfill my end."

But the man is looking for limits, and Jesus believes the commandment to love the neighbor is about love without limits. We don't just love whites or males or heterosexuals or working class people or church members. But keep in mind, too, that although the question-asker is a curious lawyer trying to justify himself — to make sure he accomplishes the checklist of "neighbor-loving" so he's "right" with God so he can get into the Kingdom of Heaven (see, he thinks it's a place you *go to*) — although the question-asker is a lawyer trying to see how far he must extend himself, *the people who are crowding around to listen to this exchange are pious Jews.*

For them there's a pecking order. Things are fixed. The clergy — here represented by priests and indirectly by Levites — would be the ones you'd surely expect to help someone. After that you'd work down to a Jewish lay person, someone who would *probably* help a stranded traveler. At any rate, the story Jesus tells would have given his hearers a delightful and entertaining surprise if he had let the priest and the Levite pass by the man in the ditch, and then had a Jewish lay person stop. It would have seemed somewhat heroic, and the hearers might have felt good about themselves. But then it would have been just a nice little story.

We need to know that the pious Jews despised Smaritans — not disliked, but avoided them almost under penalty of death. To the Jews, the Samaritans were the scum of the earth. Now recall the story. A Jew, and probably a pious Jew (since he is traveling to Jericho from Jerusalem), is set upon by robbers, stripped of everything, and left in a ditch to die. Along comes a priest, and the hearers think: a religious man like a priest will surely help a pious Jew in distress. But he doesn't; instead, the priest sees him, crosses to the other side of the road, and passes by. Next comes another person, a Levite, who was a designated lay associate of the priest. That's sort of an unordained lay pastor. He also sees the pious Jew in the ditch, crosses the road, and passes by.

It's now that Jesus' listeners expect to hear the master storyteller introduce a Jewish lay person, so that lay person can be a hero and help. But Jesus then says, along came a *Samaritan* — the despised enemy, not only of the Jew in the ditch, but the despised enemy of the Jews who are listening to Jesus' story. They're appalled. And not only does the Samaritan stop, but he goes a step further by binding up the Jew's wounds, putting the man on his own donkey, and taking him to a place of lodging where he cares for him. The next day he leaves money with the innkeeper for extended care, promising he'll pay even more if there is additional care required.

Jesus' hearers must be astonished. They are suddenly confronted with two words that seemingly *cannot* work together — good and Samaritan. Good Samaritan? And can you imagine the shift in thinking required of the Jew in the ditch who looks up and sees, through his fogginess and pain, a *Good* Samaritan? That certainly must challenge the wounded Jew's presuppositions.

But Jesus doesn't just leave those hearers hanging. you see, Jesus wants them to commit themselves in the story the way we did when we fell for the punchline of the dummy-who-said-no joke. Remember, it was then, when we found ourselves committed, that we truly found ourselves part of a changed reality.

In the Bible passage, Jesus has *described* this new reality, this image of possibility, of hope, this potential called the Kingdom of God. But he has to get his listeners to *participate* in it — even if just for a moment. They have to see and experience that there is indeed a far, far better way, a more excellent way — that the Kingdom of God isn't far off, that the Kingdom is a *present* as well as a potential reality. He's set it up, like the joke about the dummy who said "no" . . . but he hasn't gotten the dummies to say "no" yet, to fall in and find themselves confronted with a new reality, with a present Kingdom of God.

Now remember . . . the lawyer's original question was: "Who is my neighbor?" It looked as if we were going to figure out whether the man in the ditch qualified as a neighbor whom we'd be required to help. But Jesus, in the punchline, recasts the question, redirects it, and asks, not: "Was that injured man a needy neighbor?" but: "Which of these three, do you think, proved neighbor to the man who fell among the robbers?" Of course, since the answer is obvious, the lawyer quickly answers, "The one who showed mercy on him." And probably most of the other listeners, that crowd of pious Jews, were nodding their heads right along with the lawyer.

Just at that point it must have struck them — and some of them must have had very puzzled looks appear on their faces, as the question came to mind — "Did I just agree that there may be such a thing as a *Good Samaritan*?" For some of them there's an inrush of understanding, of hope, of a possible new reality called the Kingdom of God. Suddenly the world doesn't have to be the way they thought it had to be. Maybe the lion can lie down with the lamb. Maybe the weapons of war can be turned into plows. Maybe there can truly be peace and harmony. What a thought, eh? It's the *satori*, "the little point" that suddenly explodes and provides understanding and meaning. Wow!

Maybe when we hear the story of the Good Samaritan, if we are to truly hear it as something other than a Boy Scout good-deed story, we need to hear it in a modern context. Robert McAfee Brown suggests that Americans hear it as a "Good Russian" parable — with a person (an "undocumented worker") getting mugged and left for dead in a ditch only to be passed by a Presbyterian minister, then by the head of a social service agency. Finally an atheistic Russian woman clerk from the Russian embassy stops and plays the Good Samaritan.[1]

That fresh image may work, but I think it might work even better if Jesus went to a Ku Klux Klan rally and *they* asked him whom they had to include as neighbors. Jesus then might tell the parable, having the Grand Master of the Klan crash into a ditch only to be passed over by a bigoted white sheriff and a bigoted white minister who had frequently bought drinks for him. Finally, along would come a black sharecropper playing the part of the Good Samaritan.

How do you think the hearers at the Ku Klux Klan meeting would respond when Jesus asked, 'Which of the three proved to be the good neighbor?'' They'd suddenly find themselves pairing together the words "good" and "black." "The good black person." And how would they deal with that topsy-turvy reality?

A present day example may help. It very much illustrates one individual's *satori* experience, a time when the punchline exploded and created a sudden, breathtaking awareness of the possibilities of the Kingdom of God. Dee Horn, a school teacher, tells about taking her class on a trip to Paris:

We ten hungry Americans grabbed food at a French street cafe just as it was closing down. An hour later, stomachs churning, we decided to find the hotel where our luggage had been delivered and dig out our medicine kits. The luggage was there, but the rooms were full.

A sweating tour guide handed us a scrawled address and called cabs to take our group (nine high school students and a teacher) to another hotel.

One of the students had already begun vomiting. We had no time to question, no time to complain, no time to demand.

Directors could have grabbed cameras and made a movie to remember at the site of the second hotel. There was a shabby background, obvious clientele, red lights in windows blinking off and on.

The logic in my brain said: We should leave this place. You could be sued, cut out of teaching forever.

But the churning action of my stomach said: You have no other place. Stay here. Even parents will understand.

The stomach won.

Inside, the night desk clerk wore the uniform of a supervising call girl of the streets of France . . . spangled, fluffy, overbright advertisement proclaiming, What you see is what you get.

Her face told me two things: She was the Madam of the house, and I could relax. She turned and yelled upstairs in colorful French that can be loosely translated, "Hey, sisters, turn off those lights. We have real cow manure down here. Come fast and help."

For days we vomited our way through memories of Gay Paree. Those women headed out to local stores for medicines and soups, washed filthy towels, cleaned odorous rooms, hummed songs to help us sleep. As my teenaged men gained health, they tried a pass or two. But the passes were returned by lectures — lectures to curl teeth and make eyeballs roll. Those boys didn't try again.

When the tour bus came to pick us up, our tears were real. They took no funds to pay for all they'd spent. Through the trans-

lator they said, "Send cards. We want to know when you are safe at home."

Until that trip, I guess I thought just grandmothers and lifelong friends know how to help. People must be "pure" to do real good. The kids and I have changed our thoughts. From our experiences with strangers who became our family in France, we know that goodness also comes from unexpected places. [2]

I'm not sure just what might give us that sudden flash of understanding, that Aha! moment which unexpectedly and almost violently fills us with a sense of possibility, of the presence of the Kingdom of God. After all, we may believe, as those pious Jews who were listening to Jesus believed, that *we* are the brothers and sisters of the household of faith, that we are the chosen people, the privileged people of God.

What would strike us like that Good Samaritan parable, confronting us suddenly as a flash of insight, a vision of the present reality of the Kingdom of God? Maybe to see that the nourishment, the true bread of life isn't always provided by the minister or the church-going lay assistant. Maybe we need to have Communion served by a lesbian, or to be cared for in our illnesses by a house of prostitutes, or to receive lifesaving CPR from a person with AIDS. In our need, in our life together on this planet, we need to discover ourselves suddenly ministered to by an unexpected *neighbor*, a neighbor we either hate or fear — a Communist, an atheist, a black, or a homosexual. I don't know. But let's stop looking for limits, for checklists detailing whom we must love and whom we can exclude. Instead, let us be neighbors. And let us be open to the *present* reality of the Kingdom of God.

---

[1]Robert McAfee Brown, *Unexpected News: Reading the Bible with Third World Eyes* (Philadelphia: Westminster, 1984).
[2]Dee Horn, in *Alive Now*, March/April 1988, pp. 12-13 Used by permission.

The Still Small Voice

I Kings 19:1-19a

Paul Tillich, the great American theologian, said: "Our language has wisely sensed the two sides of being alone. It has created the word 'loneliness' to express the pain of being alone and it has created the word 'solitude' to express the glory of being alone."

That's elegant. And it rings true. Haven't we all, at some time in our lives, remarked at the difference between being lonely and being alone? And haven't we all felt the need to be alone?

One Thursday I was feeling kind of exhausted. It had been a week of list-making, a week of too many things to do, too many loose ends to tie up on too many different projects. Besides that, my back was killing me. But there was so much to do that I couldn't really slow down enough to rest it and let it heal.

By Thursday afternoon I had had enough, so I took my dog, jumped in the car, went to a friend's cabin a couple miles from civilization. The dog and I escaped.

Once there, I turned on the gas lights and started a fire in the woodstove. We went for a walk and, after a half hour or so, we returned to a warm, cheery, comfortable retreat.

I felt like an outlaw safe in a hideout, like Thoreau in his cabin on Walden Pond, like Walter Mitty in the depths of his own mind.

In the recliner beside the fire I fell asleep. When I awoke, it was dark. As I sat there half-asleep and half-awake in the solitude, a voice didn't *speak* to me, but it seemed to *come* to me, assuring me that I was sufficiently refreshed (at least for now), and reminding me that I had to get home for supper, that my wife and I had plans for early evening, and that I had some work I needed to finish up on my computer to take to the church office the next morning. In effect, the voice seemed to be both reassuring me and reminding me that my time-out, my escape, was over, and that I needed to get back to take care of business.

So the dog and I packed up, closed up the cabin, and headed home, a bit more rested, refreshed, and ready to take care of business

Those two things — Tillich's words and my experience of the still small voice — help me to understand a little more about Elijah's adventure.

Times are tough in Israel. Not only is there a searing drought, but there's this ongoing battle between the worshipers of Yahweh (God) and the worshipers of the Baals (the Canaanite or Phoenician fertility gods). The battle is worsened when Ahab, the wimpy king of Israel (and a Yahweh-worshiper), takes Jezebel as his queen. (She is a shrewish Canaanite woman and a Baal-worshiper).

Jezebel becomes the patron — and sort of the patron saint and protector — of the Baal-worshipers. She works hard to promote Baal worship as the official religion.

In the midst of this conflict stands the great prophet Elijah, faithful servant of Yahweh. Whenever people are tempted — particularly by the drought — to be unfaithful and fickle and to turn to worshiping the Baal fertility gods, Elijah preaches and calls them back to faithfulness. Because he is effective, he's a thorn in the side of Jezebel.

One day it all comes to a head in a contest on Mount Carmel. Elijah squares off against 450 priests of Baal. It's 450 to one — the difference being, of course, that it's really

450 priests with impotent gods against one Elijah with Yahweh, the only true God, creator of the heavens and the earth.

An altar of firewood is set up on the mountaintop, and the contest is to see whose gods or God will make the altar catch fire. The 450 Baal priests go first. They dance around, throw themselves on the ground, beat and whip themselves in a religious frenzy — but nothing happens.

Next it's Elijah's turn. But he decides to make things even tougher. He soaks the firewood with water, pours water all over it until there are troughs of water draining off the altar. He calls Yahweh to show these phonies up in a miraculous way, and after a couple of prayers, *the thing ignites.*

Elijah then, in his zeal, incites the crowd of bystanders, calling them back to faithfulness in Yahweh — and he and the crowd take the 450 priests to the Kidron Stream and cut their heads off.

Need I tell you how angry that makes Queen Jezebel? Need I tell you how much pressure Jezebel puts on her wimpy husband, King Ahab, to get Elijah? Although no all-points bulletin goes out, Jezebel does make a clear threat to Elijah, telling him she will soon see him laid out like her 450 priests.

So that's where this scripture picks up the story — at the time of the threat.

Elijah, who has been on such a high, who has just come from such a victory, who has just come from feeling he is being faithful and doing God's work, now feels depressed, alone, dejected. It seems to him that the whole country is after him, and he feels like he's the only prophet left giving a faithful Yahweh pitch. He's sick and tired of being sick and tired. Despite the big victory for him and God against the 450, his life and ministry must go on.

Jezebel seems to have accepted the Mount Carmel thing

as a minor setback, but here she is, coming at him again. Even after a big victory, no sooner is the smoke settled than a fresh round of challenges and projects faces him.

Elijah tries to escape, to retreat. He heads for the mountains in his depressed, exhausted state.

And look what happens. He falls asleep under a broom tree, and miraculously he is fed, nourished, sustained. Food and drink are placed there somehow by God, and Elijah is able to continue on his journey.

Eventually he holes up in a cave on Mount Horeb. Maybe he fired up the woodburning stove and laid out in an easy chair.

Next comes a whirlwind or a storm of some kind. But Yahweh, Elijah's God, isn't in the whirlwind. Then comes an earthquake. But Yahweh isn't in the earthquake. And then comes fire, but Yahweh isn't in that either.

All those signs are common in Old Testament stories. They are outrunners or signs of a "theophany" or a manifestation of God's presence. But those things — the whirlwind, the earthquake, the fire — are *not* God. They're just forerunners. Yahweh, Elijah's God, our God, is not to be in any way confused with the forces of nature — whirlwind, earthquake, fire — despite the fact that insurance policies commonly refer to such calamities as "acts of God." Our God is not simply the impersonal forces of nature. Our God is a personal God, one who communicates, acts, loves, comes to us.

And that's what happens with Elijah in his depression, in his cave mentality. God comes to him and communicates with him. The text says, "after the fire a still small voice." That's the phraseology of the King James Version and the Revised Standard Version. The New International Version translates it "a gentle whisper"; Today's English Version says, "a soft whisper of a voice." But those are all poetic renditions, technically incorrect, because at that point there's no mention of a whisper, a breeze, or a voice of any kind. The Hebrew actually says, "a sound of gentle stillness," or better yet, "the sound of fine silence."

The sound of fine silence. That silence — the silence after the whirlwind, the earthquake, and the fire — is so deep and penetrating that you can *hear* it. You can hear the silence. No cars, no planes, no voices, nothing. Just silence. "The sound of fine silence."

Sometimes God comes to us that way — in the perfect silence. Our intellect tells us no, but our experience tells us yes. Sometimes God comes to us in the perfect silence.

But Elijah is dejected, depressed. He has allowed his work load and his woes to become magnified, and he's fallen into the trap of the cave mentality. He has begun to wallow in self-pity.

As one commentary writer wrote:

> *Elijah had nursed his depression and vindictiveness into self-pity, one of the mind's most vicious circles. The person who goes around pitying himself bores others with the repeated story of his troubles, and the result is that he is left more and more to himself. Thus he becomes the only audience to which he can pour out his woes, and as these are poured back into himself, they foam up into an ever more bitter and intoxicating drug.*

It's then that a voice comes to him. Every version of the Bible but one says, "the voice *came* to him." Not "the voice *spoke* to him." The voice — and it doesn't say whose voice — came to him, asking simply, "Elijah, what are you doing here?"

Elijah answers. But listen to the self-pity he's developed "I have been very zealous for the Lord, the God of hosts; for the people of Israel have forsaken thy covenant, thrown down thy altars, and slain thy prophets with the sword;

and I, even I only, am left; and they seek my life, to take it away."

> *Elijah was in the cave mood . . . Both his mind and heart had gone into hiding. He was still free from Ahab and Jezebel, but he was a prisoner of himself. He had shut the sunlight out of his mind. He had drawn the shutters of his heart. When doors are slammed against us, we are prone to draw into ourselves and lock our hearts against others. Distrust begets distrust.* [1]

Then comes the voice of God. In Elijah's case he is told to get back to taking care of business. Get out of the cave mood and the self-pity mode. His strength is refreshed, his faith is strengthened, he renews his commitment, and he regains his vision. He knows what he has to do next, and he goes and does it.

If we look at what happened, it's not just similar to my experience at the cabin. We all have times when we feel overworked, overloaded, overwhelmed. We're bound to have days when we feel exhausted, depressed, alone, and under-appreciated.

But God will come to us and refresh us and renew us, because our God is not a God of thunder and lightning and earthquake, but a personal God of caring and communication who wants us to be at our best as much as possible.

In some way, what we're doing today — celebrating the Lord's Supper — is like the Elijah experience. Elijah was coming to the end of a long, hard week and was trying to get up to meeting another week. Something instinctively made him escape — partly for the practical reason that his life was in danger, but also because his well-being, his being well on God's behalf, was also threatened. On the journey, God provided food and drink — for Elijah under the broom tree, for us at the Lord's table. Like Elijah, we will be strengthened for the week to come.

But we won't only be physically strengthened, for God knows we also have need of spiritual strengthening and refreshment. Like Elijah, in the fine silence, in the stillness, in the solitude, we will be strengthened.

And finally, as happened to Elijah, a voice will come to us and give us comfort as we need it and direction as we seek it and listen for it — the still small voice of God. This is the Lord's table, and he invites anyone and everyone to join him this day and every day.

---

[1]*Interpreter's Bible*, Volume 3, p. 161.

Jesus Is Made Known in the Breaking of the Bread

Luke 24:13-35

Luke's narrative here is one of those narratives that we can easily picture. It was late afternoon on the very first Easter day, and two disciples — apparently not of the original twelve — but nevertheless, two disciples, were walking along the dry dusty road from Jerusalem to Emmaus. They were pretty down-in-the-mouth for they had just lost their messiah, Jesus of Nazareth, the one they had thought would be the Savior of Israel. So they were walking along this dusty country road, and there was no air moving at all. The flies were buzzing around and they could hear the stillness — no sounds of cars or even a distant airplane overhead. The road ahead, particularly far off a half-mile ahead, seemed to be shimmering and watery as the heat rose from it. It was hot, and they couldn't wait for the sun to go down. So they passed the time by yakking back and forth, maybe trying to straighten out their heads, trying to make sense of their grief and disillusionment.

Their leader, their Messiah, their teacher and mentor, had allowed himself to be crucified. Even when Peter had raised a sword in the Garden at Gethsemane — the night Jesus was betrayed and the mob came to take him away — even then he had made Peter put the sword away. *He had allowed himself to be taken. He had allowed himself to be crucified unjustly.* It just didn't make sense to these two on the road.

Fingerprints on the Chalice

About that time, as they were looking off at the heat pools shimmering on the road ahead, someone, Jesus, drew up from a side road and walked with them toward Emmaus. They didn't recognize him. Not even when he pointed out that in the Old Testament, in Scripture, the prophets foretold that an essential part of the Messiah's task was to suffer before entering his glory, as part of his enthronement and his mission. This traveler on the road to Emmaus pointed out to the two disciples how all the Scriptures (from Moses on) bore this out.

And when they neared the village, Jesus acted as if he were going further, but they held him back, saying, "Stay with us; the day is almost over; it's nearly dark." So he went into the house to stay with them.

Considering the nearness to suppertime, it's not surprising that they sat down to table, or that Jesus took the bread, blessed it, broke it, and gave it to them.

And then it happened — their eyes were opened and they saw clearly — their eyes were opened as surely as they were for the blind man whom Jesus had healed by the Pool at Bethsaida. It was as if the scales fell off their eyes and they could see clearly again through their grief and confusion. *Their eyes were opened and they clearly recognized him!*

And he disappeared . . .

And they arose right then and rushed back and told the eleven apostles — the twelve minus Judas who had hanged himself — they rushed back and told them what had happened on the road — and how Jesus had made himself known in the sharing of the bread.

For me, that last line sums it up: "He made himself known in the sharing of the bread." I think that Jesus is made known to us in many ways; but I think that seeing the reality of Christ in our lives happens frequently through

52

sharing meals together. In the most basic way we feel God's presence in certain events, particularly in meals.

I saw a picture recently in my hometown weekly newspaper. It was a closeup of the smiling, wrinkled face of a 105-year-old lady. She was blowing out birthday candles on a cake. All around her, almost forming a halo of faces, like the communion of saints, I suppose, were the United Methodist Women from my home church. They were the ones who gave the party and the cake for this beloved old member of the church and the women's group. I'm sure Christ was present there in the sharing of the bread (or cake, in this case). It happens all the time.

In the early church there were two kinds of Communion meals that have worked their way together into our current ritual. There was the Passover meal, a ritual meal celebrating the deliverance from Egypt by way of the Red Sea. It was celebrated with a sprig of parsley, some matzoh, and a bit of salt water. it wasn't very filling for a hungry person, but it carried a great deal of meaning because of the repeated ritual and litany. The emphasis wasn't on eating, but on remembering and being thankful.

Then there was the love feast, a real evening meal. It was more like a church supper, with a sharing of what one had. It could actually fill you up if you were physically hungry, and there was a provision that the poor be fed, too. So in a way, it was both a church supper and a soup kitchen. The emphasis wasn't so much on remembering, but was more on fellowship, common sharing, and giving thanks.

Eventually the two meals converged in the church, and we developed this Communion meal called the Eucharist, which means "thanksgiving." Giving thanks and sharing at least a little bit of food seemed to be the common point of the two meals, and the importance of ritual from the Passover meal or *Seder* was emphasized. But rather than use the Passover elements — the salt water, the parsley sprig, and the matzoh — Christians used what Jesus had used in the Last Supper in the Upper Room — simple commonly-found elements of bread and wine.

Even today in the church universal, as we celebrate the Eucharist, we find variations in emphasis from denomination to denomination and from local church to local church. Some churches, like the Roman Catholic and the Episcopal, lean more toward the importance of ritual. Others, including numerous Methodist churches, lean more toward fellowship and a shared experience, with small groups of people gathering together at the rail to take Communion by breaking the bread together.

I suspect that church suppers — both evening fellowship meals and evening paid suppers — are the result, not only of financial needs, but of deep-felt needs to experience the presence of Christ in a way more like the early love feasts.

It may be that there isn't as much meaning in the more ritualized communion meal for many folks. I don't think it's accidental that many neighborhood or home Bible studies have coffee and a snack. Even here on Sunday morning, our Bible studies follow our coffee and fellowship time.

"Jesus is made known in the sharing of the bread."

But there's another part besides the meal in today's scripture lesson. These two disciples on the road to Emmaus don't just eat a meal with a stranger. They also spend time with him on the road, breaking not only bread together, but breaking open the Scriptures, the Word of God, together. They talk about God and about the death of the Messiah. Along with Jesus, they explore what the Scriptures say about the crucifixion event and everything that led up to it. They begin to see something getting clearer.

Maybe the best comparison is to the man whose blind-

54

ness is healed in two stages. After the first part of his healing, when asked what he can see, he says, "I see people, and they look like trees walking. Things are kind of fuzzy and indistinct — but they're coming." Then, after the second stage of his healing, he can see perfectly fine. These two disciples on the Emmaus road begin to see in a sort of fuzzy way as Jesus talks with them and helps them search the Scriptures to determine what the death on the Cross means and what it means in their lives. That's the first step.

Sharing an intimate fellowship meal, sensing and accomplishing one's mission by taking in a person needing a meal, acting hospitably — that was the second step. That's when they were healed of their spiritual blindness and of the blinding confusion and grief that was immoblizing them. So the Bible study and the discussion on the road were important, too. But even then, their blindness wasn't healed. It took the whole package for the healing. It took both steps, both stages for clear vision. The study, the expounding of the Word of God, the interchange of ideas and the expressing of doubts — that was all combined with the fellowship and a sense of mission over a shared meal — to produce a healing because of the real presence of Christ.

"Jesus was made known to them in the breaking and the sharing of the bread."

And so it is with us. Now that we have heard the words of Holy Scripture, and we have heard them worked around and wrestled with, let us wrestle with them and stretch ourselves, that we might experience the first step of healing and clear vision. And let us also complete that with a Communion meal, a meal of thanksgiving together at the table of our Lord Jesus Christ. Let our eyes be opened and our hearts rejoice. Let Jesus be known to us in the breaking and sharing of the bread together.

Breakfast on the Beach

There is a handful of narratives about Jesus' appearance after the empty tomb. Several center around the empty tomb itself, like the one in which the angels say Jesus is risen, or the one where Jesus himself appears and says to Mary Magdalene, "Do not touch me, for I have not yet ascended to the Father." And there's an appearance to the disciples when he says to doubting Thomas, "Go ahead, stick your hand in my wound and be sure it's really me." Another time Jesus walks along the road to Emmaus with two disciples, probably not of the original twelve, finally being made known to them in the breaking of the bread at suppertime. Of the many strands of stories of Jesus' post-Resurrection appearances, this one about breakfast on the beach is my favorite.

Imagine. It's been some time since the empty tomb and perhaps since the other appearances of Jesus. But nothing significant has happened. Things have pretty much gone on as before. Nothing changing, no uprisings, no upheavals, maybe not a whole lot of religious conversions.

So Peter, maybe feeling a bit useless and down-in-the-mouth, decides to abandon the silly notion of preaching about the Kingdom of God, and to return to what he knows best.

He says to the others, "I'm going fishing."

Apparently the others were feeling down and useless, too, and needed something familiar to do. They declare, "We'll go with you," and they join Peter. The night brings only darkness and empty nets, though, and they head back toward shore tired, hungry, and even more downcast.

But suddenly, just as the rosy dawn begins to peek over the hills that surround the lake, there comes a voice from the beach, cutting through the mist. It's Jesus calling to them, but they fail to recognize him. It may be the morning mist, of course but it's not uncommon in the post-Resurrection stories to find that followers don't recognize Jesus at first. Anyway, Jesus yells, "Children, have you any fish?"

"Children" isn't the best translation, and I prefer the way Dr. James Moffatt translates it in his Scottish version. He uses the word "lads." I can just picture Jesus standing on the beach of Scotland's Loch Ness in the chill morning mist, from which Dr. Moffatt has him call out in a brogue, "Lads. Lads, have you got anything?"

The disciples, responding only to a voice at a distance, not recognizing either the voice or the person right away, simply (and probably glumly) reply, "No."

And the voice immediately calls back, "Then cast your net on the right side of the boat, and you will find some."

So they did, and it was so full of fish that they couldn't pull it in. At that point one of the disciples, most likely the gospel writer John, who had been extremely close to Jesus while he was alive, exclaimed, "It is the Lord!"

Apparently the incident brought to mind a similar incident back when Jesus originally called his disciples to be with him. Remember the incident from Luke chapter 5? It occurred while Jesus was still alive.

The people were pressing upon Jesus to hear the Word of God as he stood by the Lake of Gennesaret. Then he saw two boats by the lake; but the fishermen were on the shore and were washing their nets. Getting into one of the boats, which was Simon Peter's, Jesus asked him to put out a little from the land. Then he sat down and taught the people from the boat. When he had finished speaking, Jesus told Simon to put out into the deep water and let down his nets. But Simon protested, "Master, we toiled all night and caught nothing! But if you insist I will let down the nets." And when they had done so, they enclosed a great shoal of fish; as their nets were breaking, they beckoned to their partners in the other boat to come and assist them. The fish filled both the boats until they began to sink. When Simon saw this, he fell down at Jesus' knees, saying, "Depart from me, for I am a sinful man, O Lord." For he was amazed as were those with him, including James and John, sons of Zebedee, Simon's partners. Then Jesus said to them, "Do not be afraid; from now on you will catch people." And they left everything and followed him.

Back to the present text, though. It's no wonder, when the voice from shore said "Cast your net on the right side," it's no wonder John's and Simon Peter's ears pricked up. And a moment later, when they actually began dragging in fish, and when John exclaimed, "It's the Lord!" Peter could hardly help but plunge excitedly into the water, slogging toward shore with legs that felt like rubber as they strained against the water.

Yet the question remains, "Why does Peter, in particular get so excited?" After all, everyone else stays with the boat and catches up later. I think the next part of the text gives us a clue. It says: "When they got out on land, they saw a charcoal fire there, with fish lying on it, and bread."

A *charcoal fire!* You know, there's only one other place in the Bible that mentions the phrase "charcoal fire," and it's a key to answering our question about Peter's excitement. Let's look at the other place.

In John 18 Jesus is betrayed by Judas in the Garden at Gethsemane. He is led away to the courtyard, and Simon Peter, who has sworn that he would never desert or deny

Jesus, follows. But remember, Jesus said, "Before the cock crows you will deny me three times." The account begins at John 18:15:

> *Simon Peter followed Jesus, and so did another disciple.*
> *The maid who kept the door to the court of the high pri-*
> *est said to Peter, "Are you not also one of this man's dis-*
> *ciples?" He said, "I am not." Now the servants and officers*
> *had made a* charcoal fire, *because it was cold, . . .*
>
> *Now Simon Peter was standing and warming himself.*
> *They said to him, "Are you not also one of his disciples?"*
> *He denied it and said, "I am not." One of the servants*
> *of the high priest, a kinsman of the man whose ear Peter*
> *had cut off, asked, "Did I not see you in the garden with*
> *him?" Peter again denied it; and at once the cock crowed.*

I like the way Luke's gospel captures Peter's emotion at that point, saying, "And Peter remembered the word of the Lord, how he had said to him, "Before the cock crows to-day, you will deny me three times." " And [Peter] went out and wept bitterly."

Now the connection is made — the connection we see in the use of the phrase "charcoal fire" both in the court-yard and on the beach here. Try to feel, if you will, the immense weight of guilt and shame that Peter is carrying. He is, after all, Peter — the rock, the first one to make the confession, "You are the Christ," the faithful, well-meaning, loud-mouthed disciple who blurted out, "Lord, even if all the others fall away, I would give my life for you," He is Peter, the one who three times denied even knowing Jesus on the night of his betrayal. If anyone would ever be ashamed and afraid to show his face, I think it would be Peter. If anyone were ever in need of forgiveness from his

Lord, it would be Peter.

I'll bet his impetuousness is what made him leap from the boat and come sloshing ashore. But I'll bet that, as he got closer to the person by the charcoal fire, as he saw Jesus warming himself just as he, Peter, had warmed himself that night in the courtyard, as he saw that the person by the fire was indeed Jesus, Peter must have lowered his eyes with shame. How could he face his Lord?

But then what happens? Does Jesus reproach him? Does Jesus blame him? Does Jesus treat him as a traitor, as a deserter?

No. There is fish on the fire, and there is bread beside it. Apparently there was only a little, though, maybe just enough for one or two people. And just then the others arrive from the boat, six more mouths to feed besides Jesus and Peter. What to do!

But think for a moment. Where else did we see bread and fish, but not enough to go around — at least, at first glance? In Mark 6:30 we read about a crowd that was hungry, and the disciples, having only enough food for themselves, wanted Jesus to send the people away to search for their own food. But Jesus had made five loaves and two fish feed a multitude.

But what of the other beach, the charcoal fire and the seven dejected disciples? What of Peter, waiting to see if his Lord will reproach him as he believes he deserves?

Jesus says, "Bring some of the fish you just caught."

So Simon Peter, maybe trying to earn his way back into Jesus' good graces the way little children sometimes do when they've been naughty, "went aboard and hauled the net ashore full of large fish, a hundred and fifty-three of them; and although there were so many, the net was not torn." At that point I envision Peter shyly approaching Jesus, stepping up close with his eyes averted, waiting to see whether Jesus will acknowledge that he has hustled to bring over the fish to please him. And Jesus' eyes and Peter's eyes meet for a moment, and while Peter's eyes are filled with fears and tears, Jesus' eyes are soft and loving and forgiving.

But there's a pregnant pause. Peter doesn't know where he stands. His heart stops and his breathing ceases for a moment.

And then Jesus slowly smiles and offers the invitation, as he did at the Last Supper, at the feeding of the 5,000, at the feeding of the 4,000, and at all the other meals. "Come," he says, perhaps beckoning with his hand, "Come and have breakfast."

And what of Peter's sin? What of three denials in the courtyard? Maybe Peter needed to be able to act something out to counter the three denials which were so sharply etched in his memory. Maybe Jesus sensed that. That passage continues:

> When they had finished breakfast, Jesus said to Simon Peter, "Simon, son of John, do you love me more than these?" He said to him, "Yes, Lord; you know that I love you." He said to him, "Feed my lambs." A second time he said to him, "Simon, son of John, do you love me?" He said to him, "Yes, Lord; you know that I love you." He said to him, "Tend my sheep." He said to him the third time, "Simon, son of John, do you love me?" Peter was grieved because he said to him the third time, "Do you love me?" And he said to him, "Lord, you know everything; you know that I love you." And Jesus said to him, "Feed my sheep."

As we hear the invitation to the banquet this morning, to the communion rail, remember, there is no sin grievous enough to keep us from the Lord's table. We are all Simon Peters, one moment warming ourselves at the fire of denial, the next warming ourselves at his fire of forgiveness. With a soft glance, a warm smile, a gentle gesture, Christ invites us to table as he has invited so many others. "Come and have breakfast with me."

But after we have eaten and been satisfied, we must recall that we are fed so that we might serve in Christ's name. We must go forth from the meal as disciples, answering the question asked Peter, "Do you love me?"

"Then feed my sheep."

Small Church Communion

A while ago I attended a wedding at a Roman Catholic church on suburban Long Island. I had never been there before, and when I drove into the parking lot and saw the church, I was stunned. It was huge, almost twice as big as the high school I attended, where our graduating class consisted of 76 students.

Inside it was more of the same. The sanctuary was like a small cathedral and it awed me. It could seat between 1,500 and 2,000 comfortably, and the 125 who came for the wedding were swallowed up in it. The parish newsletter I picked up at the front door stated that there had been forty-one baptisms in the church — *during the month of June!* I wondered what it would be like to be a pastor there and to serve Communion on Sunday morning to a small intimate group of 1,300 — then repeat it at the second mass, and the third, and the fourth.

Let me answer that myself. It would be cold and impersonal. I certainly wouldn't know everyone by name or even be able to recognize most of them by face. As has become the case in many large Protestant churches as well, the focus would not be on true community for the Communion, but on individual and personalized religion — each person trying to get him/her self right with God. Somewhere in the Middle Ages we got headed wrongly into that direction (individuality); and later, particularly in this century

as large churches developed, things got further deperson-
lized and further away from a theme of community. it's iron-
ic that the more people there are in a group, the less it acts
as a community, and the more alone its individuals feel. I
believe the small church is the right size for worship and
for a common-meal type of Communion together, whether
it be at a table or at an altar rail, or even in the pews where
we can see each other and nod and smile and touch. I believe it so strongly — the worth of the small church, that
is — that I'd even go so far as to say that large churches
are the *wrong* size for Communion. I also believe that even
in many of our churches — large and small alike — we've
strayed pretty far from what the communion — the *eucharista* or thanksgiving meal — was all about. And that's
too bad, because our small churches are just the right size
for experiencing God in community.

Have you ever wondered what the church service might
have been like in the early days of the church? Justin, the
Christian apologist, has given us a descirption of the Sunday service at his small church in Rome around A.D. 150.

*On the day which is called Sunday, all who live in the
cities or in the countryside gather together in one place.
And the memoirs of the apostles or the writings of the
prophets [scripture] are read as long as there is time. Then,
when the reader has finished, the president [preacher],
in a discourse [sermon], admonishes and invites the people to practice these examples of virtue. Then we all stand
up together and offer prayers. And, as we mentioned before, when we have finished the prayer, bread is present-
ed, and wine with water [Communion]; the president
likewise offers up prayers and thanksgivings according to
his ability, and the people assent by saying, Amen. The
elements which have been "eucharistized" are distribut-
ed and received by each one; and they are sent to the ab-
sent by the deacons [home Communion]. Those who are*

prosperous, if they wish, contribute what each one deems appropriate; and the collection is deposited with the president; and he takes care of the orphans and widows, and those who are needy because of sickness or other cause, and the captives, and the strangers who sojourn amongst us — in brief, he is the curate of all who are in need. (Bard Thompson, ed. Liturgies of the Western Church, *Cleveland: World, Meridian Books, 1962.)*

Justin's description is of an intimate and joyful act of thanksgiving, one done not individually but in community. He doesn't speak of isolated worshipers independently interacting with the priest, each with his or her separate little bland-tasting wafer or mini-cup of juice, never casting a glance at the person beside or behind. Justin is describing a corporate experience here, a Communion of community, the action of an intimate group of believers — and perhaps non-believers or others struggling to believe or to search out their faith — who all share together, pray together, live together, and eat and drink and give thanks together. They're active, not passive, in their ministering as the Body of Christ. They have a sense of who they are *together* as the "family of God."

William Willimon and Robert Wilson don't pull any punches in their book, *Preaching and Worship in the Small Church* (Nashville: Abingdon Creative Leadership Series, Lyle Schaller ed., 1980). In a section praising the latest printed Communion materials they say:

Simply stated, these new services illustrate that contemporary liturgical renewal is taking its cue from the period before the church became big, successful, and respectable; . . . pompous, dramatic, and extravagant; . . . Directives for contemporary worship renewal are coming from a church that was then still a family, gathered around a family table, eating a family meal. (pp. 65-66)

If we look at today's scripture reading from the Book of Acts, we can see that the Communion, the Eucharistic meal, wasn't just a "religious" observance, a separate liturgy in the back of a hymnal; nor was it a separate service printed in a book of liturgies. It was the regular gathering of the *small church* to celebrate, receive, and pass on the gifts of God. Scripture was spoken from memory or read, concerns were shared, prayers were offered, a sermon was preached, a collection was taken, a meal was shared, and the needs of those who were hurting were seen to.

Doesn't that sound like our usual worship service in a small church? There was nobody off in a corner alone, meeting with the priest or "president" to drink a little of what some in the later church called "the medicine of immortaltiy." No, life and all of life's gifts were of God, Christ was of God, and these were shared in community. The emphases were not on *individual* penance or *individual* salvation, but on *eucharista* or thanksgiving, and on *koinonia* or fellowship, and on the coming of the Kingdom of God — *all experienced in community.*

In fact, in a letter to the church at Corinth, the Apostle Paul admonishes the Corinthians for distorting communion by *idion diepnon* — "eating the selfish meal" or "eating your own meal" — seeking to stuff their mouths with as much "heavenly food" as they can, rather than the communal *kurakon diepnon* or "Lord's Supper."

William Willimon, in *Worship as Pastoral Care* (Nashville: Abingdon, 1979), makes a sharp observation:

> You have heard it said that the family that prays together stays together. I say to you that the family that eats together *stays together.*
>
> Could the contemporary breakdown of many of our families be attributed to our families' so rarely eating together? . . .

little wonder that love and unity are difficult for us. We cannot share something even so basic as bread.

And if mealtimes are basic for the unity and maintenance of human families, how much more basic is this table fellowship for the family of God. Something sacred happens to people who have shared food and drink.

Wow! That bears repeating. What an incredible thought! "Something sacred happens to people who have shared food and drink."

Willimon continues:

All across cultures and faiths, the act of eating together is a universal sign of unity and love. Jesus knew this. One need only recall the progression of meals in the Gospels in which he ate with saints and sinners to be reminded of the centrality of table fellowship and the symbolic power of sharing food and drink . . . Nor is it surprising to find the early church, when it gathered for Sunday worship, gathered not in the temple but at the table. (Pages 166-167)

To you I say this: The small church has been short-changed of late, sold out in favor of the numbers game and hurt by unfair comparisons to the large church. A terrible, grievous, and unfortunate mistake has been made, because the small churches — and not cathedrals like the one I was in during the first week in August for a wedding — are the right size for meaningful worship, for genuine community, for experiential education, for lifegiving support — in short, for true, intimate, spiritual communion.

I've given you some scriptural and historical background, and I've appealed to you by intellectual argument. But there's more to be said in favor of small churches and community-style Communion. However, it's not intellectual;

it's more emotional. It's what happens in a true community on a human level. So let me close with an example that probably could never have happened in a cathedral-size church.

Ruthie attended one of the small churches I pastored in the western mountains of Maine. She was in her early fifties, though she acted more like an eight-year-old. She was described to me as "borderline retarded." Ruthie could read haltingly at the most basic level, but she couldn't comprehend what she had just read. She lived with her mother and, because she wasn't capable of taking care of herself, family members and friends in the area would look in on her regularly.

Ruthie loved being part of things, though. And Ruthie especially loved church. At church everybody knew her by name and knew what Ruthie was like.

Each Sunday when it was time to sing the hymns, Ruthie would stand between her mother and her aunt, singing along. She'd have her hymnbook open to the right page, but she couldn't read the verses fast enough to keep up. The open hymnal was so she'd be like everyone else. Usually, though, our worship service would include a song Ruthie knew by heart, and her face would take on this huge, glowing smile, and she'd really belt it out — always louder than the congregation and in her unique, shrill, off-key voice. Ruthie was definitely a character.

Thinking myself to be an innovative pastor, I decided one day to do Communion in a different, more "meaningful" way. We usually alternated between going to the rail and having it served in the pews. This time I asked folks to form a circle around the sanctuary and link hands. We would say a prayer and I'd pass the bread around, asking each person to take a piece and wait for the silver chalice to come to them. They were to then dip the bread into the chalice, eat the purple bread, and pass the chalice to their neighbor. It would symbolize Christian unity and sharing and lots of other good things.

Ruthie wasn't there just then. She and her mother were downstairs plugging in the coffee pot and arranging the cookies for the fellowship time that would follow the service. Ruthie loved to do the cookie arranging, expecially if she had those wafers that were chocolate on one side and vanilla on the flip side. That way she could use them whichever way she wanted to make lots of nifty designs.

Everything went smoothly. I started the bread to the left and people took a polite little piece each. Then the chalice got started on its way around, being passed very carefully, because the grape juice was more than three-quarters of the way to the rim. People dipped their bread and ate. We were quiet and solemn — almost somber — as if we were meeting clandestinely in the catacombs or doing something of great import to the world.

Just as the chalice got halfway around this large circle of forty people, the sanctuary doors opened and Ruthie stepped through. Her entrance placed her right opposite me. She was caught off-guard by this unfamiliar configuration. I could see the confusion in her eyes. What made it harder was that the woman right beside her had the chalice, and, without thinking, she handed it to Ruthie first thing. Ruthie had no model to follow, so she cradled the silver chalice in her hands. Her face seemed to ask, "What do I do, Pastor Steve?"

I smiled one of those too-kind, gentle-Jesus, pastoral smiles and tried to prompt her in my mildest ministerial voice, saying, "The blood of Christ, Ruthie. Take, and drink."

With that, Ruthie's eyes lit up. She looked down into the chalice, put her lips to it, and drank the whole thing!

Our jaws dropped and our mouths flew wide in disbelief! But by then she was finished. There stood Ruthie Phillips — empty chalice in her hands, a huge ear-to-ear smile on her face, and a big grape-juice mustache on her upper lip.

But what's important is what came next. The chalice kept going, kept getting passed — and each person after Ruthie *pretended* to dip his or her piece of bread in the chalice, then ate it. We joined hands, said the Lord's Prayer together, I said the benediction, and everyone hugged spontaneously. Then we went downstairs for coffee and ate the cookies which Ruthie had arranged, complimenting her on the nice patterns.

It wouldn't have happened in a large church. It happened because we were a small church and everyone knew Ruthie. It happened because of *community*.

Maybe that simple story says more about Communion than all the arguments, apologies, and treatises ever written. It works for me.

I hope this morning, as we join together for Sunday dinner as the family of God, you'll not be afraid to smile at the deacon who serves you, or to look at your neighbor beside you or behind you as you partake. And when you do, give thanks. For God's sake, give thanks . . . for that person individually and for the Communion of saints.